T0158976

Whatever Works for You

A Working Woman's Guide to Surviving a Busy Life While Maintaining Peace

Deborah McVay-McKinney

InspiringVoices®
A Service of **Guideposts**

Inspiring Voices books may be ordered through booksellers or by contacting:

Inspiring Voices
1663 Liberty Drive
Bloomington, IN 47403
www.inspiringvoices.com
1-(866) 697-5313

Because of the dynamic nature of the Internet, any web addresses or links contained in this book may have changed since publication and may no longer be valid. The views expressed in this work are solely those of the author and do not necessarily reflect the views of the publisher, and the publisher hereby disclaims any responsibility for them.

The content of this book contains actual family members of the author. All other names and characters are purely a product of the author's imagination or are used fictitiously, and any resemblance to actual persons, living or deceased, businesses, companies, events, or locales is entirely coincidental. While the author has made every effort to provide accurate information and advice, neither the author nor the publisher assumes any responsibility for the information and advice included herein.

Certain stock imagery © Thinkstock.

ISBN: 978-1-4624-0305-9 (sc)
ISBN: 978-1-4624-0306-6 (e)

Library of Congress Control Number: 2012916509

Printed in the United States of America

Inspiring Voices rev. date: 09/20/2012

For my one and only Cowboy, Pookie, and Monkey ~

your love inspires me every moment.

CONTENTS

ACKNOWLEDGEMENTS

I cannot begin to thank the many, many people throughout my life who have believed in me and encouraged me to be all that I can be.

I would especially like to thank my family, each and every one of you. I would never be the person I am without your love.

My husband Bruce has supported every project I have taken on since the creation of Time To Spare (which he also named seventeen years ago). My daughters, Dana and Megan are the joy of my life. They bring happiness to every aspect of every day.

Thank you stepmoms everywhere, especially mine, who taught me the best way to be a "second mom."

To all my girlfriends ~ and you know who you are: Amanda and Janet from the very beginning, through The Birthday Girls, the Thursday morning Bible study ladies, and everyone in-between ~I thank you for the laughter, tears, honesty, eye rolling, hugs, prayers, advice, celebrations, empty nests, saying good-bye, welcoming in, and always, always being there.

This book would not be possible without the editorial skills of Larry Allen, who told me thirty years ago that I was a good writer. He is still making me one today. Thank you for believing in me all those years ago, as you continue to do today.

I could not end this list without a special thanks to my dad, who has been a part of my life through all my good and bad decisions, who never stopped loving me, and most of all, who taught me the true value of faith.

I am grateful to you all. With all my heart, I thank you.

The Beginning

Where to begin and why now? Looking back, I started babysitting when I was twelve years old and have managed my own income ever since. I worked my way into a job as a receptionist at eighteen, moving into the public relations department the following year. Thanks to many generous people I had the honor of working with through the years at a variety of businesses, I made my way into middle management by the time I was 33 years old. Even though I also attended college, I never finished my four-year degree.

By today's standards, I couldn't even secure an interview for a management position without at least a four-year college degree. I believe I am from the last generation that could rely on a high school diploma and good work experience to get hired and be given a chance to prove myself. Our youth are not going to be so fortunate. Not only is a four-year college degree the requirement comparable to my generation's high school diploma, but a master's degree is most preferred by employers hiring today.

During the past fourteen years I have been raising my daughter, from infancy through middle school, and there have been quite a lot of distractions along the way. I became the picture of the sandwich generation when my 85-year-old grandmother was no longer able to drive, but lived an hour and a half away from me and my family of four. My stepdaughter living in another city was entering high school and my daughter was a toddler. Weekly trips to assist my grandma took over my life for several years until we finally convinced her to move closer to us.

Being the sweetheart she always was, she refused to "interfere" with our life by accepting our invitation to move in with us. When she broke her hip for the second time the following year, leaving her wheelchair bound, that choice became a blessing in disguise. Our two story home with sunken levels on the main floor would not have accommodated her needs. In addition, the other important woman in my life, my own mother, experienced several strokes, and lived out her remaining years in a nursing home three hours away.

On top of that, I decided to take my part-time small business and turn it into a full-time career. Being a home-maker, care-giver, and mother of a toddler and teen stepdaughter, all while trying to run a business, was not an easy task.

I also loved volunteering and meeting new people, especially other women ~ most importantly ~ meeting women with a strong sense of faith.

Throughout all of this time, people would constantly say to me, "I don't know how you do it all!" This always took me by surprise. For years, people have made that statement with a look of awe. Each time, I look at that person equally in awe. I always reply to that remark, "What do you mean, 'how do *I* do it all?' I want to know how *you* do it all."

People I know seem to think I never sleep, am chained to my computer (which sits in the front seat of my car, apparently, since it is also perceived that I am always on the go), can organize the most complicated set of circumstances into a magically orchestrated event with one hand tied behind my back, and can straighten out an emergency situation with my eyes closed.

So what is my life, in reality? Fortunately, I have managed to make it this far by paying attention to what works for other people and applying similar, sometimes simpler, steps to complete tasks in my own life. More importantly, I was raised by the most organized woman I could ever know, my mother. Thankfully, I managed to absorb her knack for making endless lists and checking things off, as well as her "take it as it comes" personality. I truly believe mimicking her skills and continuing to pay attention through the years has been a tremendous help in making it through each busy day.

Early in my life, my mother was a military wife with three young children, each born in a different state. No sooner did each of us come along than we were whisked off to another far away destination. Not only was my mother raising all of us before there were such conveniences as disposable diapers, baby wipes, bottle warmers, bouncy seats, car seats, and childproof gadgets galore, but she also lived in countries where the local residents did not speak a word of English.

I have to confess that my mother and I never experienced that dreamy mother-daughter bond when I was a child. I always wished for the mommy who would let me dress up in her clothes, make delicious cakes in the kitchen, and play in the park with me every Saturday. My mother, in her defense, had dreamed of finishing art college and moving to Hollywood to design evening gowns for Hollywood starlets.

As my mother told the story, it was a twist of fate for her when my dad left college in southeast Ohio one day, drove straight to Philadelphia, where my mother attended art college, and proposed on the spot, telling her he could not live without her. Romantic, yes. Worth the life style trade? Fortunately for me, yes! Much later, I found an old sketchbook belonging to my mother which included her designer gowns. Quite honestly, she should have followed her dream. If the drawings I found were any indication, she would have been a genuine success.

Rather than design dresses, my mother successfully managed our lives. The first seven years of my life, my father, brothers, and I were packed and moved into the next residence always with the greatest of ease. After that, we settled into suburbia in a brand-new Colonial-style home on a cul-de-sac filled with other thirty-something parents raising middle-class families.

Room by room, my mother went about decorating, wallpapering, and setting furniture in just the right position. Closets were organized and cupboards arranged. Grocery lists were made, coupons clipped, and dry cleaning sent out. She had her own laundry and sewing room installed in the basement of her dream house, and a perfectly manicured lawn, where she grew beautiful flowers in the front and delicious vegetables in the back. Potluck dinners, block parties, barbecues, holiday celebrations ~ you name it, my mother was ready to plan it.

However, I was a very shy child. I preferred to read in my room, or play next door with my best friend, rather than be the extrovert that was my mother. Somehow, I did manage to observe enough of her skillful personality to retain much of it.

Many women I know live very hectic lives. First to come to my mind is a mother of seven children living in the suburbs. *Seven children* in the 21st century! Married to a very busy corporate vice president, she runs her own service company. All the children are honor roll students, involved in sports and academic clubs at school. The entire family participates in a variety of philanthropic organizations annually. When I stop to count towels, sheets, and clothes, the laundry must be endless. Not to mention the cooking, cleaning, shopping, and other weekly tasks needed to maintain a large, active family. Maybe with that many children, everyone has his or her own responsibility list that must be completed in order for the family's whole world to keep from falling apart. I would love to be a fly on their wall for one day just to see how *they* do it all.

Then, there is a military wife who is alone much of the time with her small children. Being another sandwich-generation daughter, she works full-time at a busy dental practice while keeping time open for her elderly parents. Add to that, the family lives in a century home in constant need of repair. With carpooling children, running a home basically as a single mother (think about every decision to be made on her own, plus bill paying, house-cleaning, lawn mowing, shopping, cooking, laundry, helping kids with homework), getting to work on time, and responding to her parents' needs, how can she ever find time for herself? She must also worry constantly about the danger her spouse may be in wherever he is located far across the world.

The socialite woman may not have children, but she works seventy hours a week taking care of a long list of needy clients, running a huge estate which she shares with her equally busy spouse, and maintaining her role as president of her country club. I always assume this woman, who is never seen in public without being perfectly manicured, pressed, and coiffed, has no less than a dozen personal staff available to take care of her every demand. Was I surprised to learn that other than a few service providers (lawn care, etc.) this is not the case at all. She is simply extremely organized.

These women are my inspiration. When I look at each one of them, I see that they all possess a strong sense of faith. When extra busy, overwhelmed, over-committed, faced with uncertainties, and just plain stressed ~ as many of these women are on a daily basis ~ their strength comes from knowing they are not doing it alone. They rely on a higher power, along with their organizational skills. And, those words are the key to all of us living successful, stress-free lives.

Be faithful and organized and you will rule your world!

Rule Your World

First and foremost, I am a list person. If your life is super busy, has a lot of responsibilities, and more people than just you in it, you need lists!

Yes, I know, there are a hundred electronic ways to stay organized, but I am old fashioned. I have heard too many horror stories of data not backed up, electronic calendars, address books, phone directories, and such which have mysteriously disappeared from the electronic hemisphere, for me to trust anything but my datebook and a notepad.

It is so simple to keep yourself from becoming overwhelmed with things to remember. Just write it down and forget about it. But, don't forget or misplace where you wrote it down! And simply use just one book with a notepad for what? Notes! My book is the smaller 7" x 9" size with a snap closure. It contains a weekly planner, phone/address directory, and notepad.

Keep a plastic divider, which also happens to be a ruler, inserted in the binder for the current week. I use highlighter pens to track various aspects of my life. Blue is work items, orange is for my daughters, green is volunteer projects, yellow is for my personal info (haircut and medical appointments, workout schedule, girlfriend time!), and pink doubles as anything to do with my home or husband (service calls, his travel schedule, etc.) Why pink for my husband? It was the only color left in the box when I decided he needed a color, too!

I can't tell you how valuable my color coded system works for me. When it is tax time, I can easily find the days I travelled and how far, by just looking for blue. When I need to track the last time I had my hair trimmed, I look for the yellow and schedule another appointment if needed. I can tell how busy my daughter was with school or sporting activities by looking at orange. Does this sound like just too much to keep up with? Believe me, it is worth it when you need to access information about your life quickly and effortlessly.

Stop wasting time by getting in your car and driving randomly all over your shopping area. Make a list in advance and route your stops. Your gas tank and checkbook will thank you. What are you doing there, once you arrive? Again, a list of groceries, assorted gift and home needs, etc., will save you time. Once home, you can schedule friend time with that yellow highlighter, because you were organized and efficient while running errands and now have extra time on your hands.

Our minister visited recently and noticed the magnetic shopping list on our refrigerator. I told him that was our "shopping wish list." Everyone in our home is responsible for adding to it when something runs out and needs replenished. Since we all do not eat the same foods, if a box or carton of something specific empties, it is that family member's responsibility to add the item to the shopping list.

I personally do not eat rolled oats, but my husband loves them. After noticing we were out of oats, he made the comment, "We don't have any oatmeal!" My response was, "Do I eat oatmeal? No! If it's gone, number one, why is the empty box still in the pantry? Number two, why didn't you write it on the wish list, so I could buy more the next time I go grocery shopping?" Problem solved. We have never been without rolled oats since then.

After explaining this story to my minister, he said, "Wow! My wife wishes she could make me that organized."

Upon further study of our kitchen décor, the pastor noticed a wrought iron stand with a ceramic plate decorated with the date and some colorful drawings and notes added to it.

"What's that," he asked.

"Oh, that's where I put what's happening each day, so I don't have to constantly repeat myself about daily activities for our family. Everyone can take a look and be reminded themselves."

Some other friends were visiting and overheard this response. My girlfriend asked, "Do you update that *every* day?" Actually, I do. It's part of my morning routine. While the coffee is brewing, I take out my dry erase markers and update the plate before anyone else is awake in the house. (Sadly, the "pictures" are at the level of a preschooler. I definitely did not inherit my mother's wonderful drawing talent.) Each morning this process actually helps me focus on the day and wake up myself. I leave the kitchen with a light heart as I glance back at my smiley face sun holding an umbrella, or a plump snowman wearing a top hat.

Are you rolling your eyes? Are you still reading this book? Are you thinking, "There is no way that I am buying a datebook, writing everything I need to do in it, and then highlighting everything with a color I have assigned to every task and person in my life? C'mon! I could save more time by not taking the time to go to all that effort!"

Wrong!

Just try it for a couple of weeks. Then, look back and decide for yourself if you don't feel less overwhelmed, have found more free time, and realized a never before sense of accomplishment. Even if you never buy a datebook or highlighter, you can apply some of these tips with a pen and legal pad. Just one.

Some people are sticky note crazed. They write each task on one, jot a phone number on another, and make a shopping list on a third. This just would not work for me. They stick to each other, overlap each other, stick anywhere and everywhere. I cannot imagine how this keeps people organized. I would lose track of them! Make one list, glance at it in the morning, and mark things off as they are completed.

It truly is that simple.

Week of _____

(What Am I Doing This Week?)

Monday:

_____

_____

Tuesday:

_____

_____

Wednesday:

_____

_____

Thursday:

_____

_____

Friday:

_____

_____

Saturday:

_____

_____

Sunday:

_____

_____

_____

My To Do List

(Where am I going, What am I doing there, Who do I call, What needs done?)

_____

_____

_____

_____

_____

_____

_____

_____

_____

_____

_____

_____

_____

_____

_____

_____

_____

_____

_____

_____

_____

Shopping Wish List

(or, We're All Out Of . . .)

Now What Did I Do With ___?

Let me tell you about my husband.

The first time I visited him at his home, I walked in through the kitchen door. All the white wooden cabinet doors were standing open.

"Oh, did you just paint your cupboards," I asked.

He replied curiously, "No. Why?"

"The doors are all standing open."

"Well, why should I shut them," he explained, "I'll just have to open them again."

Now the first time my husband visited my apartment, he walked in the foyer and stood just outside the living room. I asked him why he wouldn't come in.

"It's so neat, it looks like nobody lives here!"

Hence the phrase, "Opposites attract."

We dated off and on for five years after that, and finally married in 1992. Obviously, a lot of compromise has taken place regarding our living standards ever since then.

Somehow over the years, I have learned to just walk by the paper piles on the kitchen desk. I look the other way from his stacks of clean clothes on top of my hope chest, which has become an extension of his dresser drawers in our bedroom. I believe he actually views all flat surfaces in our home as free space for placing pocket contents, opened mail, and newspapers. Occasionally, I move it all away to either his office or our bedroom, in the hope that someday the piles will end. And, eventually, they do manage to disappear, so I know he must have some type of system that works for him.

However, the one thing I cannot understand is the never-ending search for his keys! I have installed not one, but two, key racks by our garage door, where we always enter the house. There are various keys on it (mine, definitely), but never the set he is searching for. I just can't comprehend how a man who is so successful in business can never remember where he last placed a set of car keys. I guess if this is the worst thing I have to complain about in my marriage, I have nothing to complain about at all. But, if this old adage never applied anywhere else, it applies here. "A place for everything and everything in its place!"

Think of the time savings if you select a regular place for your pocket contents, keys, purse, gloves, planner, to-do list, umbrella, cell phone, reading glasses, ~ the list goes on and on. Your days will begin much more peacefully versus frantic moments that come from realizing you can't leave because you lost your keys.

How many times have you heard this suggestion? Set out your clothes, pack your lunch, and get your things in order before going to bed each night. Well, I don't always follow my own advice, because I am usually too tired to even take out my contact lenses before getting into bed. I will say that I always know where my keys are.

Make your life easier, less stressful, and give yourself some free time. Take this advice for once and for all: Put the things that you use on a regular basis in the same place.

Every. Single. Time.

What Season is It Again?

What do you mean it's Thanksgiving again? How can school be ending? It's Labor Day next week? Already?

So many people I know say, "May is the new December." But, what about June, August, or October? Eventually every month becomes just as busy as the next, with home, work, church, school, volunteering, and holidays all careening around us. One event just morphs into another. Everyone is equally busy with some life event all the time. Don't agree? In which month do these situations occur for you?

1. Your children mention a new school project that requires art supplies, and you just got home from the store. Or, "Six friends are coming over to make their paper mache projects tomorrow after school, if that's OK with you, Mom?"

2. Your boss just called ~ another department has been eliminated. Guess what? You get to add two more positions to

your list of responsibilities. A raise? "Why, no," she explains, "Just be glad you still have a job!"

3. Your father-in-law fell and needs to recuperate at your home for the next three months until he can live alone again.

4. The local community volunteer group needs you to organize a small fundraiser. "Really," the association president says, "It's no work at all. The committee has done this for years! They just need you to keep them on track." Translation: organize to-do lists, make phone calls, type spreadsheets, hold meetings at your home (which also means cleaning your home and making refreshments), buy supplies, publish flyers, and raise $20,000.

Be a shining star at all times. Sure, no problem!

The first thing you *must* do is prioritize. What absolutely must get done? Go back to your lists. How full is your calendar, day by day and week by week? Can you decipher it with your color coding system yet? Take a look and find something that can be eliminated if an unexpected priority comes up. Don't forget about it, though ~ move it to a week or two out on your calendar. That way, it won't be first on your mind, nor will you risk it being completely forgotten.

Now, delegate. Do you have a team at work? Are you part of one? If so, get your team together and map out the tasks that need accomplished to complete the project. Then divide and conquer.

Who is best at getting accomplished specific tasks on the list? Who wants to take on which task? If nobody wants to do any of it, jot down each piece of the project on a separate piece of paper, place them face down on a table and have each person grab one. The paper each one chooses is their new assignment ~ like it or not!

No team at work and it's all up to you? Try it at home instead. Obviously if you live alone you will have to manage by yourself or hire service providers to help. However, if you have children older than toddlers, they can help. Start with small assignments, such as emptying the dishwasher, feeding the pets, or putting their own laundry away.

There is a huge debate about whether to pay children an allowance for helping around the house. Of course this is a personal decision. In our family, if tasks are completed and responsibilities carried through, we do pay a small amount each Saturday. If something is not done, a portion of the allowance is deducted.

We look at this as a trade-off. If you're not "paying" your children, how are they earning spending money? They must ask you for money every time they want to go to the movie, the mall, or out with friends. You are paying their way regardless, so why not help build their character by making them feel they have responsibilities and are earning a paycheck for doing them well?

During a recent workshop I was conducting for a successful group of business women, I talked about how busy spring and summer especially can become. I asked who has many of these things on their calendars in mid-to-late May:

- child's sports banquet,
- company picnic,

- teenager's prom,

- summer camp registrations due,

- end of the month work deadlines,

- family wedding or shower,

- parent recuperating from an illness,

- hosting a Memorial Day cook-out,

- niece or nephew's graduation?

"Don't even talk about school being out," one woman noted, "What am I supposed to do to keep the kids from sitting in front of the TV all day while I'm at work?"

I shared a story about a high school classmate whose mother would never teach her anything, nor even allow her, to lift a finger to help with household chores. I was amazed! I learned how to sew from my mother and grandmother when I was ten years old. My brothers and I were assigned daily chores, such as setting the table and taking out the trash as far back as I can remember. And every Saturday, there wasn't a thought of going outside to play until our bedrooms were dusted and vacuumed. I learned to iron and baked all the pastries in our family at age twelve. By fifteen, I was making dinner for our family most nights, since my mom had gone back to work full-time and I could get the meal in the oven after school.

By her 17th birthday, my classmate was spending most of her time after school at her boyfriend's house, begging his mother to show her how to do the typical household tasks. She was afraid of being on her own one day and not knowing how to manage. I never understood how *she* realized that, but her mother did not. (How had her mother learned anything when she was growing up?)

When you get your children involved in running the home, it not only teaches them responsibility, it also gives them a sense of family. Children will learn the many skills they will need to be productive adults from you. And you will earn their respect and admiration, as you should.

Once your children are helping, you can take some time for yourself. Take out that yellow highlighter and schedule some "me time." It's the only way you are going to make it all work with any sense of calm. Adding time to go for a walk, read a good magazine article, have your nails done, or meet a friend for a glass of wine will make everything else in your schedule much less stressful.

During this same presentation, we talked about the fact that even though everyone loves summer, it adds to the already over-booked calendar. Maybe it's living in the Midwest, but when the weather warms up, the invitations start rolling in. I listed all the extra invitations we had received by mid-May. At that point, it was 14 graduations, four milestone wedding anniversaries, 13 teacher gifts, 22 birthdays, and one wedding. Fifty-four gifts ~ Yikes! We absolutely do *not* give gifts for all those celebrations. But, we do acknowledge each of them.

Some of the graduates are children of girlfriends or clients, who I don't know well, or in some cases, have not even met. I write a nice note of friendship to those women. I congratulate them and remind them how wonderfully proud they should be of their child. I also give them credit for all they did in raising their child to this point in life.

Other graduates receive a monetary gift. I decided years ago that it's just easier and more appreciated to put cash in a card. There is no need to run around trying to find the perfect meaningful gift and then spend more on the gift wrapping.

How much money to give is another matter.

Someone once asked me how to determine what the "correct amount" is. I think that it depends on the recipient. There are some who would be embarrassed to receive a large amount of cash, knowing they would never be in a position to reciprocate. Other people may warrant a larger amount. I base it on the length of the relationship we have with the graduate and the family. Less expensive options are five or ten dollar gift cards to restaurants, gas stations, or discount stores. These are also always useful and appreciated.

Gifts for all those teachers who helped your child reach graduation day can get really costly.

One idea that works for both younger and older aged kids is a group gift. Ask students to write letters of thanks and add all the letters to a scrapbook to present to the teacher on the last day of school. Adding a picture of the student beside each letter makes the gift more personal. Older kids can ask their friends to forward any photos taken during school events and make a slideshow. Or, just put them all on a flash drive and present it to the teacher as a group.

I know if I was a school teacher, I would not want an endless supply of mismatched coffee mugs or potted flowers every June 1st. A personal gift is much more meaningful and memorable. Even if a group project is out of the question, have your child draw a picture or write a thank you note, add a five or ten dollar gift card from someplace close to the school and check that off your to-do list. Once again, you delegated at least part of the work to your child and saved yourself time and money. All while making a lasting impression with someone your child spent a lot of time with over the past nine months.

If you have a large extended family like we do, you know how expensive birthdays can get. Our rule is that only children of elementary school age and younger receive gifts. Everyone else receives a card of acknowledgement.

At the middle of each month, I make a list of all the birthdays coming up the following month. This gives me an idea of how many gifts I need and how many cards will need mailed. I keep a supply of greeting cards on hand and take the time to sit down and write one out for each person all in the same sitting, stacking them in the order they need to be given or mailed. Instead of spending time throughout the month taking care of one special day after another, it's all done ahead of time, all at once. It becomes a simple matter of getting them in the mail a few days prior to the actual birthday.

Another time killer are those birthday parties for the friends of your children. I just love it when my daughter comes home from school with an invitation for a party three days from today. Either she was a last minute addition to the event or we are dealing with an over-booked family. I would guess the latter is more often the case.

I keep a supply of children's gifts on hand to give. Young children are fairly easy to please. Craft kits, books, games, and puzzles, are always appreciated, especially by the parents.

How many times has your child received the latest fad item as a gift only to disregard it within the week? Classic toys and games, while not always immediately chosen, will be selected long after those others are abandoned. You can usually find these items on sale when you are out running other shopping errands. If you have the funds and the storage space, snap them up when you see them. It avoids the necessity of purchasing a costly gift at the last minute. Not to mention the time you save making a special trip to the store to buy one card and one gift at a time.

Teens are not as easy. However, teenagers love gift cards. Buy a few of those in advance, too. As an added bonus, our local grocery store chain offers free fuel points when you buy retailer gift cards through their store. A ten dollar gift card to a local movie theater with a box of candy makes a nice gift and eventually adds up to free gas for you.

All this provides another opportunity to mark things off your to-do list while saving time and money. You have just purchased groceries, picked-up "standby" party gifts, earned free fuel and found more time for yourself. How much better can it get?

When it comes to weddings, babies, and showers for either, there is a multitude of gift registry options available to the happy couple. A new trend is to set-up the event details on a personal website. You can track every moment of the expectant parent's road to welcoming baby, or learning every wedding detail right down to the relationship of each member of the bridal party to the blissful bride and groom to be.

Many of these websites provide a link directly to the store's gift registry site. From there, you can locate an item within your price range, order right at your desk, and have it shipped directly to the couple. Brush your hands together and cross that off your list.

Just be sure to select a gift that shows the personal connection between yourself and the recipient, so it will be memorable.

Project Tasks

(& Who is Doing What?)

Who	Task

Chores To-Do

(& Who's Doing Them)

Who	Chore

Cards & Gifts Month of _____

(Who's Getting One & What Are They Receiving)

Date	Name	Card?	Gift Purchased

Where Did This Year Go?

Suddenly, Thanksgiving is over. You tear off another month from the calendar. Wow, how did December 1st arrive already? Talk about adding tasks to your to-do list! Here we go again.

Many of my memories of the holiday season when I was growing up are of my mom endlessly sighing. I couldn't figure out what was wrong. All I had to do was find a special gift for my parents and two brothers. By the time I was fourteen, I added my two living grandparents and my two best friends to my gift giving list. Oh, and I had to wrap them. I think around the age of seventeen, I started writing out Christmas cards for more friends. No big deal.

I looked forward to spending a Saturday in the kitchen with my mom and grandma, baking cookies and stirring the chocolate fudge. The tree was up and decorated and magically, colorful wrapped and ribboned packages began piling up under it.

Fast forward fifteen years, and all of a sudden I own a home, have children, and a career. Now all Mom's sighs started making sense. Where

41

did all these people come from on my gift list? Besides family, there are co-workers, babysitters, teachers, our minister, attorney, pediatrician, mail and newspaper carriers, hair stylist, party hosts, and two cats! So, I immediately put my list making skills to work. Who is getting what and how much is *this* going to cost us?

Are you someone who saves a set amount all year in a holiday account at the bank or in a separate space in your dresser drawer? Unfortunately, I am not. However, I do take advantage of bargains year-round. That is the first step in not going broke during the holidays.

Once again, plan ahead. If you have the funds and the storage space, shop the sales. You can pick up really nice items throughout the year that have been marked down to super clearance prices from the past winter. Obviously, this does not include food or anything that has an expiration date (batteries, most liquids, make-up, etc.).

Start by looking for scented candles (store in a zippered plastic bag to retain the scent), holiday ornaments, picture frames, cozy socks, toys, puzzles, books, gloves, scarves,—you get the idea. Store things in a plastic storage box with a lid. It really is fun when the holidays come around and you start looking through the box. If you're really organized, you may already have a sticky note with a name attached to each item. If not, take your list of people you need to give a gift to and start assigning items. Your children will enjoy doing this if you set out items for them to select for a teacher, special friend, or grandparent. You are once again sharing the work while enjoying family together time.

When it's time to wrap the gifts, this is another task you can delegate. Unless your children are too young to handle scissors, have them help with the family and teacher gifts. Who cares if the gifts aren't wrapped perfectly (isn't that what gift bags are here to cure anyway?), it's what's inside that matters. It makes the gift more special if the children are giving it and they can proudly say they wrapped it themselves. Of course, you will be using the wrapping paper and tags that you purchased at the after holiday sale in January, so it doesn't matter if the kids use too much!

Speaking of gift bags, there are so many choices available it might make more sense to just "wrap" everything in a bag. Reusable grocery tote bags and sport duffle bags are great options as a multi-purpose gift. Repurpose department store holiday bags, which seem to appear around Halloween, since most have some type of seasonal logo on them. Add decorated tissue paper and curling ribbon bows to the handles and you don't need to purchase bags at all. Another favorite is the pre-decorated gift boxes available at dollar stores in a variety of sizes to fit everything from a baby bib to a bathrobe.

The very best idea for wrapping without spending much came from my mother. One year, she wrapped all the gifts under the tree with the Sunday newspaper comics, adding red and green ribbons and bows to each package. It looked amazing! Black and white newspaper pages give a more modern look. My mom was the queen of planning ahead. She must have been saving the comic section of Sunday's paper for several months, keeping them hidden from the rest of the family.

If you don't receive the newspaper, here's another idea. Use your child's artwork. All those coloring book pages, preschool drawings, and art class paintings come in handy. You probably would not want to wrap your gift for your boss in your child's painting, but just about everyone else on your list should appreciate the uniqueness of this recycling idea.

And for goodness sake, save the most time and frustration by picking up a desk top tape dispenser at the local office supply store, along with a decent pair of scissors. You only have two hands! How are you supposed to hold two pieces of paper together on a wobbly box, while clutching a disposable tape dispenser, tearing tape off and attaching it to the paper without losing your patience? I am not quite sure.

Make holiday gift giving for children fun, too. I can't understand why a ten dollar baby doll needs to be attached inside its box like it is a ten caret diamond waiting for a jewel thief to steal it. How many wire ties, staples, tape, and screws does it really take to secure it? Save everyone frustration during gift opening time by removing all that unnecessary packaging, installing batteries, and placing the item back in the box before wrapping it. Nothing takes away a child's excitement with a new toy faster than not being able to use it because the stores are closed and you did not think to buy batteries in advance.

If you really want to get creative, make your own gift tags when giving presents to multiple people. Print labels from your computer with the recipient's name. Children too young to read will be delighted to find gifts under the tree with their photo attached. They can easily find their gifts by looking for a picture of themself.

No? Sheets of decorated gift tag labels are inexpensive when purchased at your local dollar store. My stepmom simply uses scraps of wrapping paper folded in half, adding the recipient's name to the white inside of the paper.

Next on the list are those holiday cards. With the Internet and the abundance of social media sites, is it really necessary to spend the time and money on holiday greeting cards? You just posted your child's latest sports photo on-line, along with those beach vacation pictures from last summer, so what's the point?

I know I am old fashioned because I love both sending and receiving cards each holiday season. A long time ago, I made a spreadsheet of names and addresses of all our card recipients, so I could print mailing labels. Yes, probably tacky, but that gives me the extra time to add a handwritten note inside the card, without my hand already being tired from writing out all those addresses. The kids can label the envelopes, especially if they are at the age when they love putting stickers on everything. Let them affix the stamps and return address labels, too.

My husband and I have an annual holiday party the middle of each December, so I always double the card with the party invitation, utilizing one address label and one stamp. Our friends joke about always knowing who their first holiday card will be from, since I always mail them the Monday after Thanksgiving (which means they sometimes arrive before December 1st). But, last year we actually received a New Year's Eve party invitation on November 15th. Talk about planning ahead to make sure your guests are not yet booked.

So, how are you going to get all of these things done and still enjoy the season? You guessed it! Time to take out your calendar and pick a day or two each week to tackle holiday tasks. Schedule a few hours on Saturday morning, using one block of time to decorate the tree, another to write out cards, and one more to wrap gifts.

Invite some friends over, or have your children help, and spend a Sunday afternoon doing nothing but baking and decorating cookies. There really is no need to make a dozen different recipes. If you have many favorites, write the names on slips of paper and put them into a jar. Let your children each pick one and just bake those treats. (This works well to help keep it simple unless, of course, you're that mother of seven.) Too many baked goods at the end of the day? Put them in see-through baggies, tie with curling ribbon, and give them away as gifts. Bonus: you can cross two more things off your to-do list!

The bottom line is that all the shopping, wrapping, decorating, and baking are not the reason we have the holiday season. What is important is to spend time with loved ones, reflecting on the many blessings you are fortunate to enjoy every single day of the year. The holidays come around the same time, year in and year out. It's not going to change the season by being stressed that you won't get everything done on-time.

Planning ahead will allow you time to enjoy the season. Snuggle on the sofa with your husband, kids, pet, or just a cozy blanket. Warm some hot chocolate and read a book. Watch a classic holiday movie together as a family. Get outdoors and take a brisk hike. Enjoy a shopping break and meet a friend for coffee. Volunteer at a homeless shelter. Go to your place of worship and reflect. Relax and breathe deeply.

Buy yourself the gift of peace.

Holiday Cards & Gifts

(Who's Getting One & What Are They Receiving)

Date	Name	Card?	Gift Purchased

How About Those Milestone Events?

Now that we've made it through all the seasons including the holidays, what about those milestone parties you need to occasionally plan? At some point, your child will be turning 16 or 21, graduating from high school or college, or getting married. Your parents will be celebrating their golden anniversary or retirement.

Here we go again; more chores to add to the calendar. But, not to worry, by now you are a pro with your list-making, delegating, and organizational skills. You can apply your routine for making it through the holidays, taking the same steps to ensure a stress-free, successful party.

First ask the person whose milestone you are celebrating what they would like to do. I am no fan of surprise parties. I have never even attended a surprise party where the recipient was not secretly annoyed. Not to mention the host and guests. The host must constantly worry about how to get the guest of honor to the event without that person finding out about the party. The guests have to worry about getting to the party on-time, where to park, and ensure they are not walking in at the same time as the guest of honor!

Much to my dismay, my husband has held two milestone birthday parties for me. Given his lack of talent for party planning, he did a wonderful job on both occasions. Also in his defense, I am the one who just does not like surprises or being the center of attention. Needless to say, I was very uncomfortable during both events.

So let's just not go there. Instead, ask the child, friend, parent, etc., what their dream celebration would include. If their answer is a trip around the world, problem solved! Give them the number of a good travel agent.

If, instead, their answer is a party at home, church, or the local park, that's much easier to pull off, while making everyone happy. The first step to planning any event is finding a mutually agreeable date. Then decide on the location. You'll need to determine these two things as quickly as possible after it's decided there's going to be a party. All the other plans can then effortlessly fall into place.

If you are anticipating a large event, recruit helpers. You must be the lead decision maker though, delegating tasks according to your helper's levels of expertise. Gather everyone together and first decide a theme, based on the occasion. From there, you can build your party. Choose paper or plastic tableware and theme related menu items. Again, the honoree should make these choices and you should engage your help accordingly.

There are many invitation choices, too. A simple electronic invitation by e-mail or other free websites is an easy and affordable way to get the word out. However, keep in mind that you can only use this method of invitation if you have all the potential guest's e-mail addresses. The guests must be frequent users of the Internet to receive the invitation in a timely fashion. Hopefully, your guest of honor will be able to provide the e-mail addresses to you. You can also easily create a document invitation on your computer, copy and mail them. Again, I like the old fashioned way, which is mailing them. Who doesn't like to open their mailbox and find a party invitation in-between the junk mail and bills?

The most stressful part of planning any party is determining the actual number of guests who will attend. Nobody seems to understand the meaning of "R.S.V.P." And that is nothing new! "Regrets Only" is another problem. Are they really all attending, or did they just forget to tell you they are not? If you add a respond by date on the invitation, you would think that should clearly indicate that you are seeking a response: yes or no.

Quite a few people I know feel that R.S.V.P. indicates that the host only wants to know if you will in fact be attending. If you are not, then there really is no need to tell them. They feel that since they did not actually acknowledge receiving the invitation, then the host should assume they are not attending.

I have always thought this to be a simple matter of being considerate. It doesn't take much time out of your day to send a quick e-mail, text, or voice mail message saying you will or will not attend the party. Think about how difficult it would be if all your potential guests handled your invitation in this manner of not responding at all. How in the world are you, the host, supposed to calculate the amount of food, beverages, and other party items needed, if you have no idea how many guests to expect?

Of course you can make a party as simple or as elaborate as you wish. A simple party includes an invitation, location, some background music or other entertainment (games, movie, etc.), light refreshments and beverages with paper plates, napkins, and cups. Voila! Attendees are there to celebrate something special in the life of the guest of honor anyway. They usually are not there to critique your immaculately clean home, taste in décor, or expensive party decorations.

An elaborate party, of course, includes a much more extensive decorating scheme incorporating your party theme, hired entertainment, catering, bakery, photographer, etc. Take out your planner and schedule a task or two each week. Do not wait until the day of the party to begin shopping, cooking, and cleaning. You will be exhausted before the event even begins!

Spend the party day morning ensuring all the last-minute details are completed. Then, focus on yourself. Take a nap, read the newspaper, select the perfect outfit, and be relaxed and ready to enjoy yourself. You deserve it.

Your guests and your honoree will thank you when you appear calm and collected, ready to celebrate the special occasion. And, you will be remembered fondly long after the party has ended.

Party Planning Event Date: _____ Place: _____

(& Who is Doing What?)

Task	Who/Where	What
Theme		
Invitations		
Decorations		
Florist		
Menu		
Bakery		
Caterer		
Beverages		
Rental Items		
Linens		
Photographer		
Party Favors		
Set-Up		
Clean-Up		

What Vacation?

Do you ever dread the time everyone in your family starts talking about a vacation? It's not uncommon, especially if you are the vacation planner in your home. Here we go again, adding a whole new list of to-do items to your schedule.

You know the routine: choose a destination, make travel arrangements, find hotels, book airline tickets, reserve a rental car, determine all the things to pack, calculate expenses. And last but not least, fulfill everyone's requests for what they would like to do upon arrival at the vacation destination. Great! Ready to go?

This is simply an extension of the special occasion planning method. Vacation is supposed to be a special occasion after all. Just be sure to take steps so that it is also *your* special occasion, not simply more work for you.

If you are vacationing with your family and/or another group, plan a meeting to discuss details with everyone. Take notes of preferences. What does everyone want to include, which types of restaurants do people like, and what mode of travel do they prefer?

Now it's time to delegate. You should not have to research every option. If your children are old enough to search the Internet, assign them the task of finding out about all the places they would like to go. What is the cost, do you need advance tickets, where is it located in relation to your hotel, and is it family friendly for everyone in your group? Have an adult make the travel arrangements and someone else decide on a hotel. A teen can research restaurants by specific menus and costs.

Make a list of what you need to pack. Where are you going? Do you need hot weather extras such as sunscreen, bug spray, an umbrella, sunglasses or sun hat, a light jacket, and comfortable walking shoes? Or are you travelling during the cold months and need a parka, boots, gloves, hats, and thermal socks? Again, the sooner you get started with your plans, the less stressful it will be for everyone involved in the trip ~ including you ~ when your travel date approaches.

And don't forget arrangements for your pets, mail, plants, and lawn care, while you are gone. With everything arranged in advance, you can be ready to enjoy a relaxing vacation without the pressure of last minute things previously forgotten or not planned out. The day before you leave can best be utilized packing last minute items, double checking plans with pet sitters, and breathing a sigh of relief that you are ready to go.

Last year, our family took an eighteen day vacation, driving across the country and back. We left Ohio on a Thursday morning and within an hour had drained the car battery for no apparent reason. Fortunately, we were able to locate a Chevrolet dealer close by for recharging (the plug in cooler, laptop, and cell phone chargers had been the culprit) with little delay. Road construction just outside Chicago delayed us another two hours. By the time we pulled into our guaranteed reserved hotel at midnight, we were exhausted. Unfortunately, they were overbooked and had given our room away! Not a great first day, but we made the most of it, laughing at all of my "expert" pre-planning, still winding up in unpredictable situations.

Unable to locate another available room in that town, we drove another ninety miles, and pulled into a beautiful hotel that looked promising. The desk clerk must have felt really sorry for us because she took one look at me and said, "How is $99 for the night? And, our whirlpool opens at 6am!" I am sure the going rate was at least $300 a night, so it was one more blessing in disguise for the start of "Our Great Western Vacation" which we later nicknamed, "See the USA from Our Chevrolet."

The next morning when we started out, I was inspired with a fresh idea to lighten our trip. I thought it would be fun to ask people along our way one question and record their answers. I simply asked, "What makes you happy?" It had to be the first thing that popped into their mind without debating their answer. My sweet teen daughter said without hesitation, "You of course, Mom." (That's my girl!) My husband said, "The two of you, naturally." (That's my guy!)

First stop, the pancake house across the street from our luxury hotel. Our frazzled waitress was training a teenage girl who just could not quite understand the job description of a waitress. Not once, but three times, my husband asked the girl for a spoon so he could stir his coffee. We had to give her credit through, because throughout the remainder of our meal, every time she returned to our table, she had no less than ten spoons in her grasp asking, "Did you ask me for a spoon?"

The best question was when she came by a little while later and asked if we were ready for our check. We had not yet been served our meal! This overly stressed girl finally stopped coming to our table and was replaced with her trainer, a nice looking woman, probably in her early forties.

I thought I would spring my question on her.

"Can I ask you a question," I began. She raised her eyebrows and I asked, "What makes you happy?" Without hesitation, a wide smile spread across her face as she relaxed and answered, "My daughter! She's 15 and I have one on the way. He's a surprise!" I almost cried at her joy. What a wonderful way to re-start our western adventure.

So, obviously all the planning in the world may not provide you the exact vacation you thought it would turn out to be. But, with some flexibility and a positive attitude, it can be more than what you had dreamed. Trust and believe and you will experience more than you ever thought possible.

Probably one of the best pieces of advice I ever received about vacation time was to take an extra day at the end of your vacation once you return home. You definitely do not want to return to the office, or jump back into your children's activities and other commitments, when you are staring at a pile of mail, a mountain of laundry, and an empty refrigerator. Take the first day home to tackle these tasks and ease back into your regular weekly routine. If you do this for yourself, you will be able to relive your vacation time and time again with a happy heart full of wonderful memories you made. And, you will actually look forward to planning your next vacation with great anticipation.

Vacation Plans Dates:

Location:

(& Who is Doing What?)

Who	Task
	Travel (Air, Car, Cruise line)
	Hotel(s)
	Activities
	Restaurants
	Directions
	Packing Lists
	Budget
	Pets
	Mail & Newspapers
	Plants, Lawn Care

Sinking in Paper Quicksand?

Now that you have perfected your calendar, delegated responsibilities from your workload, and created an organized life for yourself and your family, what's next? How about better managing all of those papers that just seem to multiply on their own around your home?

If you have ever been overwhelmed and taken the initiative to tackle the paper pile-up, you have probably read a book or two containing the same exact suggestions. Touch it once and decide ~ react, file, or trash. Why do they all say the same thing? Because it works!

Why open a piece of mail, add it to a pile of past mail, documents, newspapers, etc., and think to yourself, "Hmmm, I need to respond to that someday." If it warrants a response, put it where you will actually respond to it. If it's a bill that needs paid, have a separate space for unpaid bills. If it's junk mail or other correspondence that does not interest you, have a recycling container nearby and put it in there, immediately.

If it is an item that needs attention at a later date, put it in a pending file or box. Do not put the container where you will never notice it again.

Instead, locate the time noted in your planner when you have scheduled handling pending projects and address the paper at that time.

Need to file the paperwork? Consider that with the capabilities of the Internet, most papers can be replaced if needed. Certainly, I am not an expert on finance, nor an accountant, so be sure to check with your professional before destroying anything official. If you have a scanner, use it to scan important documents, file them on a flash drive, and place it in a fireproof box. Then you can discard your documents, avoiding the paper pile altogether.

Honestly, you do not need to save every receipt. Why would you keep the stub after you pay for your monthly newspaper or trash collection? If you paid on-line or by check through the mail, you have proof of payment. What's the point in retaining and filing a paper copy? Of course, it is a great idea to keep a paper shredder near your paper recycling container. Unfortunately, identity thefts lurk everywhere, so better safe than sorry: Shred it!

Speaking of bills, do you pay them as soon as they arrive? I find it to be a better system to place all the bills in one location, along with your checkbook, stamps, and the free return address labels that constantly arrive in the mail. If you pay your bills over the Internet, one bill container is useful for keeping them together. The first and fifteenth of the month are bill paying days. (Yes, they are scheduled in my planner.) I also take that opportunity to balance my checking and savings accounts and follow-up on any pending financial matters. I don't even give bills a second thought the rest of the month.

What about magazines, books, and other forms of print entertainment? Many churches and schools seek these items as donations. Ask at your church if they support a needy neighborhood. Ask the soup kitchens in your area if they are willing to take donations. People who need free meals certainly do not have the funds to purchase current magazines and books.

Another option is the paper recycling bins located around many towns in school parking lots and shopping centers. When you recycle your papers there, they earn cash for non-profit organizations, including churches, schools, and other services for those in need. It is so easy to lend a hand to someone less fortunate. This is a simple way to give back to your community. As a bonus, you will feel relieved to have eliminated some of the clutter that causes anxiety in your life.

School has ended for the year once again. Here comes the big locker clean-out! All the artwork from an entire school year, graded papers, projects, notebooks, broken binders, and torn folders are brought home. Why can't children just throw them away at school? I suppose it makes the school custodial staff much happier by sending it off with the students.

Again, sort through the supplies, retaining reusable items for the following school year, and throw away the rest. Have your children sort the papers and artwork and decide what they would like to keep. Remind them that someday they will grow up, move into their own home, and become the proud owners of these keepsakes.

I used to make scrapbooks and would diligently glue all the A+ papers, cute drawings, and lunch notes in them. Well, the busier life became, the further down the priority list that process moved. Now, I keep all these papers in a plastic tote box covered with a lid with the school grade and year permanently marked on the outside. They are stacked neatly in a corner of the basement, ready to send along with our daughter when she moves into her first home. (And remember, the discarded artwork can also be used for wrapping paper during holidays and special occasions if you simply cannot bear the thought of recycling it.)

Do you work from both home and the office? Sometimes I find the amount of documents which need transported from one meeting to another, to my office, and home, becomes cumbersome and disorganized. I recently found vinyl tote bags with canvas straps on the outside that file folders fit in perfectly. Finally, I found a system that works for me so I can organize papers and files into a project tote, which I can quickly grab on the go. No longer are papers mixed in with those to be sorted at home or within other work projects. After sub-dividing project files into categories and labeling them accordingly, life once again became much simpler.

Think about this the next time you decide it's just easier to pile it all up and set it aside for another day. Pretend you are moving next month. What would you do with those papers? Wouldn't it make your move easier if they were already organized, in place, or thrown away? Yes it would!

Yes, You Do!

One of my least favorite phrases is, "I don't have time." Have you secretly been saying this to yourself throughout this book? Well, to that I just want to shout, "YES, YOU DO!"

Let's face it. Everyone has time. We all have the same 24 hours in every day, each day filled with the same 1,440 minutes. It's how we each decide to spend those minutes that make a difference in how we view our time.

I am a firm believer that if something is really that important in your life, you will make time to ensure certain things happen. For instance, I am constantly told that, "It's amazing how you remember everyone's birthdays and actually hand address cards and get them in the mail on time to recognize the date. I just don't have time for that."

Again, where is your list? Do you own a calendar? Are you active on social media sites? If you have any of these tools, you will be reminded of birthdays and other special occasions. The least you can do is type a quick message to someone on their special day on the Internet when it reminds you that the special day *is today*. It truly only takes one-half of one of your 1,440 minutes.

Plan ahead. There are plenty of 49 and 99 cent cards available. The dollar stores usually sell them two for a dollar. Buy a bunch the next time you are out and about and keep them in a box or a drawer where they are easily accessible. Grab that stack of thank you notes you've been meaning to tackle and write them out while you wait for your child to finish her soccer practice. Go one step further, addressing and stamping them while your son is finishing his piano lesson. Drop them in a mailbox on your way home and breathe a sigh of relief. You are done with something that has been weighing on your mind for weeks.

When it comes to adding projects to your to-do list like organizing friends for a night out, there is always someone (usually more than one) who says, "Can't you plan it? I don't have time."

Again, "YES, YOU DO!" It's just easier to claim you don't, so someone else will take the task on, letting you off the hook. Even the most organized person would like someone else to make the arrangements once in a while. How many minutes does it take to email your social group and ask which of two dates and two venues are the preferred? One? Once everyone replies, you hold the power to make the decision, if you take this on! Use another one or two of your 1,440 minutes to send a confirming email to everyone with the plan details. If you really want to show you care, Google the venue for a phone number and use up one more minute by calling to make a group reservation. Ta-dah, you just earned a gold star within your circle. You also proved to yourself that you *do* have time for something other than the usual daily tasks in your life. Not to mention, you have a fun event to anticipate.

One of my favorite things to do as long as I can remember was to listen to my grandmother tell me stories of her early married life. My grandmother was born in 1915 and married in 1934. The following June, my mother was born. By 1935 when she came along, the United States was in the worst phase of the Great Depression. Being a newlywed and a first time mother, in such dire economic straits would be enough to put any of us over the edge today.

I would spend hours analyzing how my grandmother could possibly handle all the day-to-day duties of homemaker, wife, and mother, especially during a time in history when there were none of the "modern conveniences" that we are spoiled with now. No car seats (if you were fortunate enough to have a car that decade), disposable diapers, prepared baby food on the store shelves, or formula powder to mix with water. Where was the baby when the laundry needed done, clothes hung on the line to dry, ironing, cooking, baking, gardening, vacuuming, cleaning, ~ the chore list goes on?

Grandma would explain that there was simply always family around to help. Has it really only been two generations ago that families all lived in the same neighborhood, or at least in the same town? Children played in the streets, ran through corn fields, walked to town, and rode their bikes in the country. And nobody worried or thought twice about not being within constant eyesight of their children. It was definitely a different time.

My grandparents lived with an aunt and uncle who owned a boarding house during the Depression. Times were especially hard in the far eastern side of Ohio during that time, when the primary employment was coal mining and factory work. As the economy faltered, so did the jobs in those depressed areas. Grandma told about the older people who came to live at the boarding house who simply had nowhere else to go. I have always pictured this home as a normal family residence that just happened to be debt-free, so was opened for rooms to rent.

Grandma was responsible for handling the laundry and ironing of all the boarders. The washing machine was located down a narrow flight of stairs to the basement and the clothes were hung out to dry, then every piece brought back inside to hand iron. This included sheets and other linens! I always imagined the basement door or back door standing open and my mother crawling and falling down steps. "No," Grandma would explain, "You see, everyone was assigned a task, including the boarders. Their job was to care for the children."

I just love that picture. A big comfortable living room just inside the wrap around front porch lined with rocking chairs, and filled with people of various ages, all enjoying just being together. Life was hard during the Great Depression, but in many ways, it was also much more simple and peaceful than today. I never imagine anyone uttering, "I don't have time for that." If they hadn't known it prior to those years, everyone soon realized that dependence on each other and their faith was the ultimate importance in life.

So what's important in your life? If your answer includes your family, friends, peacefulness, stress-free moments, relaxing, having fun, and making fond memories, I hope you have learned some new ways to enjoy all of these with the advice I have shared.

My wish for you is a rewarding, full life, filled with peace and happiness.

AFTERWARD ~ THE EULOGY

A tribute to the two women who nurtured, inspired,
and shaped me into the person I am today.

My mom's mother, Esther, passed away at the age of 95 just six weeks before her own passing. All at once, both my mother and grandmother were gone. All my life, these two women guided me into the person I am today. I can't remember a time when I did not hold them both in my heart, taking their advice, learning a lesson, or sharing a happy occasion.

However, they were very different women. Grandma was the definition of a lady. She adored her role as wife, mother, and homemaker. She could prepare meals that would melt in your mouth. Growing up and even into my 20's and 30's, Grandma always seemed to be wearing an apron and standing near a stove. Our favorite dish was her mashed potatoes. My daughter and I have a favorite line in a movie where the mother says to the grandmother, "These mashed potatoes are so creamy." Every time we eat mashed potatoes, we recite this line. However, every time, I also think of my mother and grandmother. Mom loved Grandma's meals, especially her creamy mashed potatoes.

Grandma showed me the correct way to prepare so many dishes. She taught me the proper way to manicure my fingernails. Somehow, I complained every time I had to help with the yard work at home, but I loved working side-by-side my grandparents, as we pulled weeds or raked leaves together.

On the other hand, Mom was more of a tomboy her whole life. She loved being outdoors, enjoying the beauty of nature. I loved listening to her stories of her childhood, where she ran after the chickens on her grandparent's farm. I used to make her tell me the story of how she was playing in a construction site one time and jumped onto a board with a nail sticking out of it. She said she walked the whole way home with that nail pointing out of the top of her shoe and the board slapping the ground. When Grandma opened the door and saw what happened, she fainted on the spot! Mom preferred to read rather than cook. She loved going to the movies. She absolutely loved a celebration.

My mother allowed me to explore books and movies that probably were too advanced for my early teen years. We would prop up our pillows in her bed on Saturday mornings and read together. Through Mom, I read *Payton Place, The Exorcist, and Helter Skelter.* We also discovered Steven King, Danielle Steele, and epic stories such as *The Thorn Birds.* The last series we read was the *Twilight* saga. I remember going to see everything from *Mary Poppins* and *The Jungle Book,* to *Love Story* and *Jaws* with Mom at the movie theater. When the *Twilight* movies came to the theater, Mom asked if we had seen them and how they turned out. I reminded her that the movies are never as good as the books and she hadn't missed much.

Mom was spontaneous, too. Many times during my teen years, my dad and brothers would be away on a Boy Scout camping trip. Often, one or more of my girlfriends would sleepover. One time about 9p.m., Mom jumped off the couch and said, "Who wants Chinese food?" We piled in the family station wagon and drove to the all-night Chinese restaurant for egg rolls and moo goo gai pan.

Another time, we were watching "Chiller Theater" on TV around 11:30p.m. one Friday night and Mom said, "Girls, how would you like to wallpaper?" She turned on the stereo and we sang along as we proceeded to wallpaper the entry hall and stairway leading to the second floor into the middle of the night.

Mom loved music. Many times I remember driving somewhere with Mom and singing along to the radio. She had a beautiful voice and I especially loved hearing her sing along to "You Make Me So Very Happy" and "You're Just Too Good to Be True, Can't Take My Eyes Off of You."

Every time a holiday rolls around, I can't help but think of my mom. She made every single holiday into a special time for our family. There were noisemakers for New Year's, Easter egg coloring in the spring, decorated bikes for the annual 4th of July block party parade, and much fussing over the Thanksgiving turkey.

But her favorite holiday had to be Christmas. No matter who came to visit each Christmas, Mom always made a point to hang up a homemade stocking for everyone. It was always fun to see what everyone brought to put in the stockings, too. I remember one Christmas in my early 20's, someone had put lottery tickets in each of our stockings. Nobody actually hit the jackpot, of course, but it was a treat!

And even after all the decorating, cookie baking, gift giving, and washing dishes were done, my favorite memories were of our family gathering around the kitchen table to play gin rummy or Monopoly. Mom would bring out the crackers and her famous dried beef cheese ball, the Christmas candy and cookies, and we would play games for hours.

I learned many lessons from my mom. She taught me to sew and we even had a sewing room my dad built in the basement. I made many of my clothes starting when I was about 12 years old. Something I carry with me today is advice Mom gave me about taking my time. She said, "Don't cut corners, Debbie. They always show." Of course, she was telling me this because I would pin the seam, but would never take the time to iron after sewing. This advice comes to mind just about anytime I start a new project. I try my best to complete projects as thoroughly as possible. Because, yes, Mom, taking shortcuts always shows.

One of the last things Mom asked me during her last week was, "Will you make me something to wear?" I asked her if she wanted a dress or skirt and she just stared at me and shook her head no. I told her I would think of something.

This request stayed with me all through the week and I finally realized that even though her wishes had always been to be cremated, she was remembering all the special occasion outfits I had made for the two of us through the years. I made her a beautiful lavender dress to wear to Jeff's wedding in the early 1980's. I had made my own wedding dress in 1992 and Dana's baptism gown in 1998. She wanted me to make something special for this occasion, too.

Mom loved bright colors and patterns. She always accessorized with bold jewelry and new shoes. So, what could I make her to help her look beautiful as she entered eternity, I wondered all that week? Finally, I decided. Mom always loved the look of silk scarves. It was with love and care, and yes, no cutting corners, that I sewed the edges of this red paisley silk scarf together in Mom's memory, just for this special day. Of course, she is not actually wearing it, but she still looks radiant.

People ask me how I learned to be so organized. I can also thank my mom for that. I have never met anyone more organized than she. As long as I could remember, Mom was making a list ~ for grocery shopping, errands to run, and chores to do. She could organize a drawer or cabinet no matter how small or how much had to be put away.

I always look back with regret that I do not have any baby clothes, books, or toys from my infancy. Then I remember my mom was a young wife, traveling with a two year old son and an infant daughter to France, where my father was an officer in the US Navy. My mom was left to care for her young children in a far off country where they spoke a different language. I am sure keeping track of mementos was the last thing on her mind.

Mom loved that part of her life, though. She told me many times these were the happiest memories of her life. She loved an adventure, she loved to travel, and those times definitely fulfilled her heart's desires.

My mother would always tell me that she was born in the wrong generation. She wished she would have been born in the 1950's and become a free spirit of the 1960's and 1970's. She dreamed of being a Hollywood costume designer. I don't know whatever happened to it, but I remember once thumbing through one of her sketchbooks of evening gowns and I have to say, she would have been a success from what I saw. Mom used to tell me that she never wanted children. When I would repeat that to friends, they would comment what a mean thing to say. I never thought so. I knew my mother well and she would have been happier had she not felt "stuck" in the 1950's "June Cleaver" role in which she lived.

She was an extrovert to say the least; outspoken and never afraid of controversy. As a shy pre-teen, I would often times be embarrassed by her out-going, boisterous personality. As I grew into an adult, I learned to love that most about her. She was not afraid to stand up for what she felt was right.

Not to say that our mom wasn't a great mom. As with every aspect of her life, she tried to make everything she did into a fun time. She always took the time to talk, laugh, and help us be our best. She supported us in our good decisions and our bad. She was so proud when Jeff would score a winning run in baseball or touchdown in football. I saw the absolute pride in her eyes when I joined The National Honor Society during high school. And, no mother could have been prouder of her son, when Larry earned his Eagle Boy Scout award. Mom absolutely adored her grandchildren. Her favorite role later in life was being Grandma to Megan, Nick, Zach, and Dana. She always wanted to know what they were doing and when she could see them again.

My mom struggled with her faith as long as I can remember. She loved the Lord, but felt her whole life that she had been surrounded by people who proclaimed their love of God, but did not live so. "They sure can talk the talk, but sure don't walk the walk," Mom used to say. At times, she would say this about me and she was right. We had our struggles later on, but I know now that was due in large part to her grief over the ending of her marriage to our dad, who she had known most of her life.

I was 25 years old when my parent's marriage ended and I remember Mom telling me that because she had supported me her whole life (which she had), now it was my time to support her. I did my best all the years since, even after she accused me of being too much like my dad to want to be around me. I was actually proud to have agreed with her—I am like my dad in many good ways. There were several years that followed when my mother and I did not have much of a relationship. I am always grateful that we did reconcile our differences before Mom moved to California in 1990 to fulfill her dream of living near the ocean and starting her life over.

My husband and I did our best to care for Mom after her initial stroke in early 1996, by moving her back to Ohio and helping her get back on her feet. By the middle of the following year, additional strokes had taken away Mom's ability to think as clearly. Having always been so close with my brother Larry, she asked to move south to be near him. Mom once again moved away, months before my daughter was born. I felt abandoned and even though we saw each other several times over the next few years, it wasn't the same close relationship I had always had with her. But, Grandma was still there for me and she taught me how to care for my infant daughter.

The years passed, and by 2003, Mom was living in Newark and we had moved Grandma into assisted living near our home in Akron, after she had broken her hip and was confined to a wheelchair. Neither of these strong-willed women ever went back to the comfort of their own homes, but both were well cared for by loving providers.

It occurred to me many times as I looked back over the past decade how these two women seemed to have switched roles with me. It was definitely my time to look in on them and make sure they were happy. Given their health conditions, I truly think that they were.

Grandma used to say to me, "I don't know why the good Lord doesn't take me home." And I would always say, "You're still here for us, Grandma. We just haven't learned everything you have to teach us yet." The lessons I continued to learn most from her were patience, kindness, and compassion. I witnessed these traits in Grandma right up to the end of her life.

Even though I could not visit Mom as often as I would have liked these last five or six years, she always had a smile for me when I did walk into her room. She would ask about Bruce and Dana (if Dana was not visiting her with me). Mom wanted to hear everything going on in my life. It wouldn't take long, though, and Mom would get tired and revert back to the past, easily becoming confused about where she was and asking when she could go home. I would always end our visit by asking if she needed anything. She would sigh and tell me no. I know Mom wanted to ask me to stay a little longer and I always wished I could.

I worried about Mom when Grandma passed away. She was sad that her failing health prevented her from attending her mother's funeral, as she had her father's in 1993. I think it finally made her realize what her life had become and she started dreaming of a better life in a better place.

She longed to once again taste her mother's home-cooked meals and feel the big bear hugs her dad always had waiting. She wanted to wear pretty clothes, feel healthy, and walk in the outdoors.

As heartbreaking as our final moments were together, I know that Mom has gone on to that place of peace and happiness. I envision the parties she is planning, her delight in the taste once again of those creamy mashed potatoes, and her good health that has been restored. I can see her beautiful smile and hear her contagious laughter.

When I went to Mom's bedside that last night, she looked at me and said, "I don't want you to ever leave me." I told her that I was right here and I was not going anywhere, no matter what. I told her she would always be with me and I would always be with her. I said, "I will miss you Mom. But it's time to go. Be with Grandma and Grandpa. I'll see you again." And I will someday. In the meantime, I know my mom is a part of me that I proudly carry in my heart, and I always will.

In loving memory of
Esther Eileen Kirtley & Carol Lee McVay
November 6, 2010

~~~~~~~~~~~~~~~~~~~~~~~

Notes

Notes